Theory of the Hashtag

Theory of the Hashtag

Andreas Bernard

Translated by Valentine A. Pakis

polity

First published in German as *Das Diktat des Hashtags. Über ein Prinzip der aktuellen Debattenbildung*. © S. Fischer Verlag GmbH, Frankfurt am Main, 2018.

This English edition © Polity Press, 2019

Polity Press
65 Bridge Street
Cambridge CB2 1UR, UK

Polity Press
101 Station Landing
Suite 300
Medford, MA 02155, USA

ISBN-13: 978-1-5095-3893-5
ISBN-13: 978-1-5095-3894-2 (pb)

A catalog record for this book is available from the British Library.

Typeset in 12.5 on 15 pt Adobe Garamond by
Servis Filmsetting Ltd, Stockport, Cheshire
Printed and bound in Great Britain by TJ International

The publisher has used its best endeavors to ensure that the URLs for external websites referred to in this book are correct and active at the time of going to press. However, the publisher has no responsibility for the websites and can make no guarantee that a site will remain live or that the content is or will remain appropriate.

Every effort has been made to trace all copyright holders, but if any have been overlooked the publisher will be pleased to include any necessary credits in any subsequent reprint or edition.

For further information on Polity, visit our website:
politybooks.com

Contents

v

A Sign of the Times

The triumph of social networks over the last ten years has also been a triumph for the keyword. Ever since Twitter and Instagram introduced the "hashtag" – in 2007 and 2010, respectively – a form of organizing statements and documents that not long ago was restricted to highly specialized professional circles has characterized the everyday use of media. In what contexts, then, did "keywords" play a role just a quarter-century ago? Something like this concept was approximated in the library and archival sciences, which, since the early twentieth century, had been developing increasingly standardized "subject catalogs" in order to make it easier to locate documents. Elsewhere, they featured in historical keyword or catchword research, a subdiscipline of linguistics concerned with analyzing the formative expressions of a given epoch or political movement. Both of these venues, however, exist on the margins of academia, and thus it can be said without a doubt that the category of the "keyword" had occupied a rather inconspicuous position before the turn of the twenty-first century. It was the establishment of the hashtag that quickly shoved this niche element into the spotlight of our present-day media reality. Today, every Twitter feed and Instagram post provides further testimony to the collective indexing or "keywording" of the world, which can be undertaken by any user of these social networks as a creative act that is unrestricted by preinstalled standards or hierarchically tiered modes of access.

In the early years of the "World Wide Web," as is well known, documents could only be connected to one another through a system of "hyperlinks." Highlighted in advance, certain words or passages of a text would lead, when clicked upon, to another place on the same website, or to a different website altogether. In many respects, the transition from the "link" to the "hashtag" as a defining networking principle was a major shift in the digital organization of statements. First, it meant that every internet user could create links independently and without any knowledge of programming, and thus it paved the way for the highly touted "social" and participatory era of the internet. Second, it meant that a method for creating links had been endowed for the very first time with a typographical element of its own. The prefixed symbol "#" – known as a "hash" in British English and as a "pound sign" or "number sign" in American English – transforms words into networked keywords. The hashtag and the letters immediately following it thus have two functions: they are both a component of visible tweets or Instagram posts and a trigger for the invisible procedure that links them together.

In linguistic terms, the hashtag thus exists on the threshold between text and metatext, and it draws the previously hidden steps of cataloging and indexing out into the open. As a binding element between everyday communication and computer code, it has become the most popular signature of the present, and its effectiveness is most clear to see in the fact that the pound/hash sign has since begun to appear beyond screens and displays. The # symbol can now be found in the titles of recent novels, on T-shirts, on signs held at political demonstrations, in graffiti, in advertisements on the side of the road and even in tattoos. In a world made of stone, paper, cotton, and skin, the hashtag cannot be clicked on and it cannot link to anything, but even on these materials it can represent a pledge – a pledge to be seen, find an audience, and pool interests. Thus the # is no longer a purely functional sign – for some time, in fact, it has also been a promising social symbol. It stands for the production and accumulation of public attention.

The hashtag is implemented so widely in today's media reality that it is easy to overlook the elementary effects that it has had within the past few years on the order of statements and on the structural principles of debates. The following book, which is concerned with the origin and the diverse social effects of the hashtag (and the # symbol in general), is an attempt to close this gap. First published in 1956, Theodor W. Adorno's famous article on typography begins with these words: "The less punctuation marks, taken in isolation, convey meaning or expression, . . . the more each of them acquires a definitive physiognomic status of its own."[1] A good 60 years later, it is time to consider the "physiognomic status" of the hashtag in today's digital culture, and particularly to consider the extent to which this symbol has influenced such things as the use of language or the creation of collectives.

The subject of my book is the remarkable career of the # symbol in the history of media. Here, I will examine how the "keyword" was used before the hashtag entered the scene, and I will discuss the symbol's most prominent areas of application during the last decade (political activism and marketing). Finally, I will look at the ways in which the hashtag has influenced socio-political movements. For it was this last aspect that, at the beginning of 2018, provided the impulse for the following considerations. It was around this time that the "#MeToo" movement took shape and incited a global, epoch-making debate about sexual violence – a debate that, over the course of several months, generated thousands of daily tweets and dozens of articles in newspapers, online portals, and blogs. The positions and legitimations of this debate have since been discussed in all of their facets; in the meantime, "#MeToo" has become a common expression and can now be found in the content pages of news magazines as a self-explanatory rubric. So far, however, hardly anyone has asked about the extent to which the media and linguistic circumstances of this debate have influenced the development of its content. To what extent, for instance, do the recurring misunderstandings and conflicts between its participants about the definitions of "harassment" or "abuse" stem from the specific way that they have used hashtags to organize their statements? For, when the various and diverse voices sharing their experiences with sexual violence all do so under the same, identity-forming keyword – "#MeToo" – this only serves to strengthen the very tendencies toward homogenization and leveling that have received so much criticism within the debate itself.

The hashtag, which has seemingly contributed so much in recent years to the formation of the public sphere, brings statements together and forms collectives. At the same time, however, it also smooths over differences and thus obscures subtleties that do not conform to a single neat rubric. This book is an attempt to fathom the power of a symbol that, until recently, was no more than a mysterious typewriter key or button on a telephone.

2

Hashtags and the Dispersion of Statements

It is generally believed that the history of the hashtag began with a tweet on August 23, 2007. On that day, the Californian internet activist and product designer Chris Messina asked his followers what they would think about using the hash sign to indicate groups of topics on Twitter: "how do you feel about using # (pound) for groups. As in #barcamp?"[2] The example that he cites – which thus happens to be the first Twitter hashtag ever used – refers to the milieu in which the idea originated. The open conference format of "Barcamps," which Messina co-founded in 2005, is distinguished by its non-hierarchical proceedings and real-time coverage on social media. One can assume, then, that his new proposal for organizing Twitter posts was inspired by his desire to support the communicative practices of Barcamps.

Two days later, Messina clarified his reasoning on his blog *Factory Joe*: "I do think that there is certainly some merit to improving *contextualization*, *content filtering*, and *exploratory serendipity* within Twitter."[3] As two other hashtag theorists have already underscored, the symbol was initially meant to function as a "coordinating mechanism."[4] Today, Messina is referred to as the "inventor of the hashtag" in numerous works on the history of digital culture, as well as in his own social media profiles and on his own websites, even though this clear attribution is somewhat misleading. In 2007, Messina at first referred to the hash sign attached to a keyword as a "channel." Even his blog entry from August 25 of that year bears the subtitle "A Proposal for Twitter Tag Channels." The designation "hash tag" for this new organizational element (at first, it was written as two separate words) was first proposed a short time later by the computer scientist Stowe Boyd, who was familiar with the # symbol, which was usually called a "hash" in his line of work, from the programming language C: "[T]he name," as Boyd recalled in an interview, "came from programmer culture."[5]

Like its name, the function of the hashtag was also conceived by multiple people working together in a "thought collective" – to borrow a term from the scientist and philosopher Ludwik Fleck. During the summer of 2007, which was one year after Twitter's launch, various internet activists and the company itself were occupied with the question of how to organize the ever-growing and unstructured mass of tweets. For instance, on August 21, 2007 – two days before Messina made his now-famous suggestion – an employee of Mozilla Firefox from Michigan, named Les Orchard, posted the laconic tweet "Twitter needs tags."[6] To this day, his tweet has received just a single "like." A day later, Orchard too elaborated on his idea in a blog entry,[7] but his post did not have anything like the effect of Messina's contemporaneous remarks, which emanated from the epicenter of digital culture at the time.

Yet it was not only such parallel ideas that made the emergence of the hashtag a more complex process than any that could be attributed to one "inventor." For, by that point, the # symbol had in fact already had a long history in the organization of online communication. In his blog entry, Messina referred to "internet relay chat," an early, text-based online chat platform whose communicative channels were based on hash signs and keywords. He thought it might be a good idea to transfer this existing classification system to the new format of "microblogging," and he also mentioned a short-lived competitor of Twitter called Jaiku, which was already using the hash sign to group topics together in 2007. As an epochal innovation, the hashtag thus emerged from a nexus of inspirations and references, and it is probably due to the marketing talent of a product designer and the need for histories of media and technology to tell clear origin stories that, today, one and the same name will pop up on tens of thousands of websites when the words "inventor of the hashtag" are typed into a search engine.

Regardless of how original Chris Messina's proposal might have been, in August of 2007 it hardly gained any traction; for some time, the use of the hash sign on Twitter remained a quirk shared by just a few friends on the site. The typographical element first began to receive greater attention in October of 2007, when devastating forest fires broke out in the vicinity of San Diego. Images of the fires were being posted on Flickr under the rubric "SanDiegoFire," and Messina urged people on his blog to use this in their tweets as a "hashtag," as he was now calling it. More and more users followed this suggestion and, by the end of October, the hashtag #sandie gofire was spreading like the fires themselves. This also had something to do with a function called "Track," which the company had introduced four weeks earlier. The service enabled users to receive updates on their phones related to specific topics by sending text messages to Twitter such as "track NYC" or "track Steve Jobs." At this point, that is, the company itself was beginning to promote the thematic (instead of author-directed) networking of tweets.[8]

By the end of 2007, hashtags had become a regular component of Twitter posts, and the microblogging service eventually overcame its initial indifference to the new element: "Enough people started using them," according to Biz Stone, one of the company's founders, "that [. . .] Twitter decided to embrace them."[9] As of April 2009, every profile page now showed a list of "trending topics," and this soon became synonymous with a list of the most frequently used hashtags. A few weeks later, the company finally introduced a function that automatically linked hashtags and allowed users to view all the tweets related to a given keyword by clicking on one.

With this innovation, which was made available on July 2, 2009, the hash sign became a defining feature of Twitter. It happened at a time when the political protests in Iran catapulted the first non-American hashtag – #iranelection – into the list of trending topics, and Michael Jackson's death on June 25 of that year prompted record numbers of posts on a specific topic. Indexing the world with hashtags was on its way to becoming an established act – a process that, with the launch of Instagram in October 2010, also spread to the publication and classification of images and videos. In 2013, the American Dialect Society elected "hashtag" to be the "word of the year," and in 2014 it was accepted into the *Oxford English Dictionary*. In an interview conducted on the tenth anniversary of his historic tweet, Chris Messina claimed that, in digital culture, the hashtag had become the "lingua franca for labeling content."[10]

This book's point of departure is the following question: what sort of changes has the spread of this new "lingua franca" entailed? Within a decade, it has fundamentally transformed the order of statements and documents – their linguistic, media-technical, and social organization. In order to describe this process more accurately, it is helpful to revisit Michel Foucault's analyses of the history of science and his ideas about the "laws of distribution" that govern what can and cannot be said within a particular thematic field at a given place and time. Foucault's method unravels historiography's traditional nodes of investigation – such as "author," "work," "influence," or "origin" – and seeks to identify a more refined and unbiased basic unit of historical analysis. In his methodological treatise *The Archaeology of Knowledge*, which was first published in 1969, he referred to this unit as a "statement." When analyzing the statement, according to Foucault, it is necessary to "determine its conditions of existence, fix at least its limits, establish its correlations with other statements that may be connected with it, and show what other forms of statement it excludes."[11] His approach is thus defined by its strict relationality; it replaces the

14

vertical, hermeneutic ambition to detect the binding meaning of individual statements with a horizontally oriented type of investigation: "I have undertaken, then, to describe the relations between statements" – as Foucault summarized his method in *The Archaeology of Knowledge* – for, he added, "there is no statement in general, no free, neutral, independent statement; but a statement always belongs to a series or a whole, always plays a role among other statements."[12]

It is apparent that the success story of the hashtag – and the everyday practice of indexing involved with it – have strongly influenced the "relations between statements" in today's media reality. What are the implications of the # symbol with respect to the clustering and subsumption of knowledge? What does the hashtag favor as an organizer of feelings, opinions, and expressions (their ability to be located and classified, their concentration around certain themes), and what does it restrict (their uniqueness, their idiosyncrasy, their inability to fit into a rubric)? When Foucault writes that a statement "always belongs to a series or a whole" and that it is necessary to "establish its correlations with other statements," one could say that, today, the intellectual work of the historian has been taken over by the automatic organization facilitated by social media and by the hashtag in particular. Around 50 years ago, it was necessary to upend the archive and its traditional categories such as "author" and "work" in order to acquire a new analytic category like the "statement"; in the case of Twitter and Instagram, a single click is all that is needed to arrange posts according to a keyword and not according to authors or the "work" of their profiles.

Thus, by explicitly exhibiting the mode of their connection, the hashtag makes it easier to see the relations between statements – the "systems of dispersion," as Foucault called them.[13] Moreover, the keyword marked by the hash sign corroborates Foucault's central definition of the "statement." In *The Archaeology of Knowledge*, he repeatedly remarks that, for historical analysis, it is not the semantic content of this unit that is of primary interest but rather its "function"; as he envisioned it, discourse analysis is not a "semantic investigation."[14] The inclusion of the hashtag in Twitter or Instagram posts can be described in precisely the same way: its power derives from the distribution of statements and documents in a strictly functional sense, one that is independent of the meaning of the tweets or photographs in question. A post may be relevant, competent, poignant, or factually correct, but this plays no role whatsoever in its ability to be networked by means of a hashtag. The software tool makes decisions according to its program and not by conducting hermeneutic assessments on an individual basis. Previously fleeting categories such as "attention" or "resonance" have thereby become quantifiable in the countable accumulation of posts and in the "trending" of particular keywords. Precisely for these reasons, it can be helpful to investigate the automated default settings behind the formation of today's knowledge and debates – for an investigation of this sort should shed light on the law that governs the distribution of statements, a law that for some time has been consolidating in a single typographical element. Today, the hashtag is in every sense the premonitory sign of discourse.

3

The Biography of a Symbol

The few linguistic studies that have been devoted to the hashtag make a point of stressing its categorial novelty as a linguistic element. In their current usage, according to Paola-Maria Caleffi, hashtags are "linguistic items whose identity does not match any part of speech in the traditional sense of the term." Oscillating between text and metadata, between signifying and networking, hashtags "are both words and not yet words."[15] More detailed information about the special nature of this symbol can perhaps be provided by its history. Where did # first appear? In what contexts did it acquire its meaning, and on what platforms did it secure its status as a fixed element of typography?

In American English, as mentioned above, the symbol is known as a "number sign" or "pound sign" (which is the term used by Messina in his tweet). These terms already offer a few hints about the symbol's early applications. Both uses began to appear in printed books around the middle of the nineteenth century, with the prefixed # designating "number" (e.g., #10) and the suffixed # designating "pound" as a unit of weight (e.g., 10#).[16] This latter use, according to Keith Houston, provides "the most credible story behind the evolution of the symbol."[17] It is the story of a centuries-long transformation that resulted in the stabilization of sloppy writing practices. For a long time, the Latin term *libra* or *libra pondo* "a pound by weight" was abbreviated as *lb* in ledgers, recipes, delivery orders, and contracts. This abbreviation entered the English language in the late Middle Ages, and it was then often written, according to a common scribal practice at the time, with a line crossing through its top to mark it as a contraction (℔). The symbol continued to be used in written documents through the seventeenth century, even by Isaac Newton himself.[18] According to historians of typography, the transition from ℔ to # was a process of ongoing refinement; in manuscripts from the nineteenth century, for instance, the pound sign already appears as a standard-ized crosshatch in notes written by accountants, cooks, and pharmacists. Over time, a single symbol emerged out of two lower-case letters with a line crossing through them, and became a common feature in printed books by the second half of the nineteenth century.

Of course, additional applications of the symbol are not hard to come across: editors use it when proof-reading to indicate that a space should be inserted in a text; physicians use it as shorthand to denote a bone fracture; and it is used in chess notation to denote a checkmate (here it is thus a symbol of interruption and not, like the hashtag, a symbol of connection). These areas of use, however, are limited to specific professions or technical language. In musical notation, the "sharp sign" has a slightly different form and is regarded as an independent typographical element – ♯ instead of #. In the United States, at least, the symbol mostly meant "pound" or "number," and in the last quarter of the nineteenth century it became a standard typewriter key. First produced in 1878, the Remington 2 typewriter introduced the arrangement of letters, numbers, and sym-bols that, at a conference of stenographers held in

Toronto in 1888, would be declared the "universal keyboard," which has remained almost unchanged to this day. Here the # symbol was located, as it is still located on American keyboards, above the number 3 on the upper left.[19]

For the subsequent career of the pound/hash sign, its inclusion on the universal keyboard was important because, at least in the United States, the # element became part of the most exclusive typographical inventory. Aside from numbers and letters, the Remington 2 keyboard contains just a dozen punctuation marks and special signs. This canonical status was then perpetuated in the early twentieth century by the development of new devices and methods for data processing, such as the standardization of the punch card system, which IBM patented in 1928 and which includes # among its 80 letters, numbers, and symbols. Media-historical references such as these are significant because appeals to tradition happened to play a decisive role in the development of the very communication device that would make the hash sign a familiar symbol in Europe as well: the touch-tone telephone.

In 1963, the American company AT&T introduced the first telephone that, instead of having the customary rotary dial, functioned with a ten-button keypad arranged in a three-by-three matrix of numbers, with the 0 placed below the 8 in a fourth row. The change from the rotary dial, which had been introduced at the beginning of the twentieth century, to the new dialing system may have offered customers greater comfort, but it was primarily motivated by a technical reason. Tone dialing, after all, made it possible to send a signal directly to the addressed apparatus instead of having to go through the nearest telephone exchange, which had been the case with the pulse-dialing system of rotary phones. This technical change increased the networking capabilities of individual telephones, which could now be connected to external devices such as answering machines or to the computer systems in government agencies, banks, and corporations. With tone dialing, it would essentially be possible to spy on conversations, receive computerized wake-up calls, and transfer money by entering a credit card number.

In the first design of the touch-tone telephone, however, these ancillary applications were not available for everyday use because, among other things, it lacked a way to confirm when a caller had finished punching in a series of numbers. Since the early 1960s, however, researchers at AT&T had been working on adjusting the telephone's design to the newly available signal technology. Prototypes were installed in hospitals and offices, and in 1968 the company presented its new model, the "Western Electric 2500," which had two additional buttons in the fourth row of its keypad, one under the number 7 and the other under the number 9. The star sign (*) and the hash sign became standard features of the touch-tone telephone, which has been the standard phone in every American household since the 1970s and in every household in Europe since the middle of the 1980s.

Douglas Kerr, a former telecommunications engineer at AT&T who contributed to the development of the touch-tone telephone, has written two blog posts about how the two new signs were chosen and named. "There had long been interest," he recalls, "in the introduction of 'codes' beyond those for the 10 digits that could be used as syntactical elements in protocols through which costumers could control emerging new and sophisticated telephone system functions." He also remarks that this development was accelerated by the "emerging relationship between telephone sets and computers."[20] The function of the hash sign as one of two non-numerical signs on the keypad was at first to confirm the entry of telephone numbers, account numbers, or credit card numbers – its purpose, that is, was to signal the end of meaningful data and issue a command to send this information.[21] Kerr's recollections are especially informative about why the # symbol was chosen at all. In the earliest versions of the 12-button keypad, the input button on the lower right was in fact a diamond sign. Shortly before the Western Electric 2500 was released in 1968, however, the symbol was swapped out on account of a decision that had been made 80 years earlier. Because the diamond sign, according to Kerr, "did not appear on most typewriters, it would be very cumbersome for the administrators of systems for the entry of data from Touch-Tone telephones to prepare instruction sheets or manuals!"[22] The hash sign (like the asterisk on the lower left side of the keypad) fulfilled this criterion, but there was some debate at first about what it should be called. For the release of the new telephone, the engineers wanted to devise a new name for the hash sign.

One proposal was "octotherp," which refers to the eight free ends of the symbol's four strokes, but this suggestion faced immediate resistance.[23] (The word has largely been forgotten by English speakers.)

With the arrival of the touch-tone telephone, the hash sign began to play a generally prominent role in the history of technology. In the words of the media historian Jeff Scheible, it signified "a promise of innovation" in that the button on the lower right of the keypad made it possible to connect every private telephone to a complex network of devices and computer systems.[24] "Please enter [this or that number] followed by the pound [or hash] key," a friendly entreaty made by automated telephone systems, is familiar to anyone who owned an answering machine or called a bank or rental car company just ten years ago. Writing in newspapers or magazines, cultural critics have long been bothered by automated forms of communication and by the ousting of real telephone conversations by computerized voices and push buttons. In 2003, for instance, Christian Kämmerling wrote a long, lamenting, and even prophetic article about this process of alienation. The end of his piece, which focuses on the # symbol as a "navigator of modernity" and appeared four years before Chris Messina's tweet, reads as though it could be describing the current ways in which Twitter and Instagram are used, especially if the term "pound sign" is replaced by the then-unknown word "hashtag." "Everything will depend on the pound sign," Kämmerling wrote: "We will enter into the world and our birth will be confirmed by the pound sign. We will get married, and instead of saying 'I do' to one another, we will simply push the pound sign. We will end our life, which will have been a single chain of commands between the star key and the pound key, with a final push of the pound key."[25]

On the touch-tone telephone, the # symbol is a sign of pure functionality; as in the early programming language C, which was developed at the same time and even in the same research laboratories, the pound/hash sign did not signify meaning but rather represented an input command (at the end of a series of numbers on the telephone and at the beginning of an instruction in the programming language). Up until the end of the twentieth century, the hash sign did not (in semiotic terms) have any semantic content but rather only syntactic content in the processes of communication technology. It was only during the early era of the internet (with its "internet relay chats") that the use of the symbol began to change. In these online forums, as mentioned above, the hash sign was used to indicate themes. Even in this new role as an indicator of keywords, however, the # did not have any semantic connotations; rather, it remained a passive element that took over certain taxonomic tasks in addition to its function as an input sign. Only during the last decade, in the form of the omnipresent hashtag, has it increasingly intervened in semantic processes and did it become the hybrid that it is today: part network command and part symbol of collectively amplified speech.

4

Where Was the Keyword
Before the Hashtag?

If the greatest effect that the hashtag has had on the laws governing the distribution of today's statements and documents is the fact that it has made the keyword a central element in the organization of knowledge, then it must be asked what roles the processes of indexing or "keywording" had played before the revolutionary rise of digital culture. Where was the keyword before the hashtag? What function did it serve in the formation of the public sphere and in the arrangement of archives? Who created it, and which operations were responsible for its dissemination?

As I mention at the beginning, the first place to look in this context is at the library sciences. As a way to document book collections, discussions about "subject catalogs" started in the United

States during the last quarter of the nineteenth century, when the first public libraries were being opened there.[26] In Europe, this form of indexing came to be established, after many individual experiments undertaken in the nineteenth century at state and university libraries, during the first third of the twentieth century. As a principle of organization beyond the author and title of a book, it began to compete more and more with the older "systematic catalogue," which had been in use since the eighteenth century and which assigns each book a place within a system organized according to scientific disciplines that, in the words of the German library scientist Heinrich Roloff, "is arranged into an intricate set of subcategories and is established before the work of cataloguing begins."[27] The "keyword," which is not confined to any single scientific discipline and which follows the organizational principle of the alphabet alone, seemed to be a more open and practical form of cataloging to the librarians debating the matter in the 1920s and 1930s. During the following decades, state libraries and large university libraries in countries such as Germany abandoned their systematic catalogs and replaced them with the new format.

"The subject catalogue," as one author observed in 1982, "currently occupies the chief position in library cataloguing."[28]

What, then, are the defining features of "keywords" as they are understood in the library sciences? In his frequently reissued textbook on subject cataloging, Roloff stresses that keywords "specify the substrate of the content of the books being catalogued. The keyword is the shortest factually relevant expression for the topic represented in an individual book."[29] According to Agnes Stählin, who created the first extensive subject catalog for a German university library, the purpose of the keyword is "to generate correct ideas in the user about the content of particular books."[30] The problem with this new organizational principle, however, is that the great freedom that it allows for cataloging entails a degree of arbitrariness as well. Because "keywords" no longer classify the content of a book according to the concepts of a pre-established system of knowledge or according to words in its title, the method is at risk of straying too far from the standards of verifiability and comparability. After briefly flipping through a book, what one librarian might consider the "substrate" of its content will depend on hermeneutic effort, and thus on a degree of subjectivity. Under these conditions, how is the new cataloging format supposed to function in an authoritative manner? For the users of a library, what is there to guarantee the objectivity of a subject catalog?

Librarians have been pondering these questions ever since the "keyword" was introduced as a unit of organization. On the one hand, institutions and universities have published detailed rules for designing their catalogs.[31] On the other hand, standard lists have been created in an attempt to ensure that the same books are cataloged in the same way by different libraries. Individual leeway should thus have little to do with the assignment of keywords. "Since 1923," according to Roloff, "a standard list has existed for American public libraries." In its edition from 1966, the list of subject headings used by the Library of Congress in Washington, DC, which also sets the standard for most university libraries in the United States, already contained more than 250,000 entries.[32] Since the 1950s, various guidelines have also been created in Europe, and these have increasingly been standardized with the help of electronic data-processing. In 1986, a committee

formed by the German Library Institute published its *Regeln für den Schlagwortkatalog*, a
nationwide set of cataloging rules, which, now
in its fourth edition, consists of 773 sections
crammed into 300 pages.[33] Since 1988, moreover,
this same institute has been publishing a so-called
"Schlagwortnormdatei" ("Subject Headings
Authority File").[34] In France, a very similar set
of rules is called "Répertoire d'autorité-matière
encyclopédique et alphabétique unifié"; Great
Britain, like the United States, uses the "Library
of Congress Subject Headings" – systems which
are intended to guarantee a procedure that, in the
jargon of library science, is known as "terminology control."

On the basis of this concept, it is possible to
describe the relationship between the keyword
(as it came to be used as a cataloging principle
during the twentieth century) and the hashtag
(as something used to organize statements and
documents). Affixed to a hash sign, keywords
on Twitter or Instagram are not subject to any
centrally regulated "terminology control" whatsoever. A few syntactical restrictions aside (no
spaces or punctuation, for instance),[35] any given

word or phrase can be turned into a hashtag. In contrast to the enduring efforts of librarians to standardize the practice of assigning keywords, to normalize the language of catalogs, and to ensure that those who do assign keywords have certain professional credentials, the use of hashtags knows no such authority. Social media allow the rampant proliferation of hashtagging. Instead of rules and "authority files," the organizational principle on social media is a specific symbol – # – that determines, by virtue of software settings, what is a keyword and what is not. In the context of the hashtag, debates about authorization or about the standardization of content are irrelevant. Every user of Instagram and Twitter is free to index things however he or she pleases. Over the past few years, the expansion of the sphere of people entitled to assign keywords in our digital culture has often been described as an act of political emancipation, and it is this that lends the hashtag its potential to create political resistance and oppositional public spheres.[36]

One hallmark of the hashtag, then, is the complete absence of any overarching regulatory authority. A second difference between the hashtag and earlier forms of indexing is the altered relationship between a keyword and its object of reference. In archives and libraries – and the twentieth-century debates about catalog systems left no doubt about this – the keyword is subordinate to the book or document that it classifies. "While reading," according to Heinrich Roloff, "the librarian seeks to find the shortest, most succinct linguistic expression for the subject of a book."[37] One could say that the substrate of a keyword is the supplement of the work that it represents. The extent to which the hashtag has changed this representational relationship becomes clear at first glance. No relational hierarchy exists between a tweet and the hashtag that it contains. The keyword attached to a hash sign is not simply a classification added later on; often enough, the relationship is inverted. That is, tweets or pictures uploaded onto Instagram are often a reaction to a popular hashtag, and people hope to take advantage of this popularity for their own posts: "A user who observes the rise of a compelling trending topic micro-meme," according to a study published in 2010 on Twitter hashtags, "may be inclined to take the tag associated with the meme and compose his or her own tweet on the subject. Thus, it is overwhelmingly likely that they might never have written the tweet if they had not been inspired to participate in the micro-meme phenomenon."[38] The hashtag inspires tweets, and this dynamic creates a different temporal and causal relationship between a keyword and its matter of reference. In library catalogs, every new book title requires a keyword; on social media, every new hashtag generates as many posts as possible.

Third and finally, this generative power of the hashtag is also associated with a previously unfamiliar amalgamation of text and metadata. The format of the catalog, for instance, is clearly differentiated from the library that it represents. A keyword is used to register a book and make it identifiable within a library's collection, but it never becomes a *part* of the book. In the case of tweets, however, signifying texts and metadata are fluidly and inextricably interrelated. The series of letters designated with the # symbol is not only part of the post (and often inserted in the middle of a sentence) – in cleverly composed tweets, it also refers to the post itself, expresses an implicit commentary, and ironically questions that which is being said.

The absence of authority, a redefinition of the referential hierarchy, and the inseparability of text and metadata: these three factors clearly distinguish the function of the hashtag in the way that statements and documents are organized today from the history of the keyword as it has been used in the library sciences. As mentioned above, however, there is another branch of science in which the category of the keyword has played a prominent role: a subdiscipline of linguistics that, since the early twentieth century, has been known as historical keyword or catchword research. In this context, the term does not play a taxonomic role but is rather understood as a means to describe the substance of a historical epoch, or the key message of a political agenda. According to Friedrich Lepp, whose 1908 study on the keywords of the Reformation is one of the foundational works in the discipline, "one measure of the greatness of an age and the profundity of its intellectual issues is the number of keywords that a period of time exhibits. . . . In their compelling brevity, they are the truest characteristic expression of an epoch's essence."[39]

In historical keyword research, too, the search for authoritative definition criteria is as old as the scientific method itself. How is it possible to discover the "characteristic expression of an epoch's essence" in any verifiable way? What are the defining features of a keyword, and what is its particular applicability? An early answer to these questions was provided by the Viennese historian Wilhelm Bauer, who published an article in 1920 about the keyword as a social and psychological phenomenon of intellectual history. "When a word transforms into a keyword," Bauer wrote, "it distances itself from its original conceptual basis." Such words, he went on, "are suddenly roused from the lexical tranquility in which they had hitherto reposed. . . . They are thus transferred from their factual and logical stage into a phase that is emotional."[40]

"Emotionality" would in fact become one of the defining criteria in the methodology of historical keyword research, especially as it has been practiced in Germany since the 1960s. In an extensive study from 1982, for instance, Wulf Wülfing identified six features of epoch-defining keywords: abbreviation, emotionalization, anti-rationality, indeterminable content, apparent clarity, and the compulsion to repeat them.[41] As recently as the year 2000, a methodological dissertation about the historical keyword cited its "emotional charge" and "appellative use" as two of its central "indicators."[42]

In light of the origin story of the term "keyword," this constant focus on "emotionality" is interesting in two respects. First, the meaning of the term in historical linguistics is the exact opposite of its meaning in the library sciences. There, since the early twentieth century, the keyword has served an organizational and cataloging function and has thus stood for a principle of rationality. The "emotional content" of the keyword, which has been a central feature of its linguistic application since Bauer's time,[43] has no role at all when it comes to organizing inventories of knowledge. Second, this concentration on the "emotional charge" of the keyword is especially noteworthy in relation to the hashtag. For what significance does "emotionality" have today in the practice of assigning keywords on social media? In the technical process that, following the instruction of a computer code, automatically turns every sequence of letters affixed to a hash sign on Twitter or Instagram into a "keyword," the category of "emotion" is obsolete. Even if the most effective hashtags do arouse feelings of empathy, solidarity, or identification (#Icantbreathe, #JeSuisCharlie, #BlackLivesMatter, #MeToo) and thus fulfill Bauer's and Wolter's emotional criteria, the network logic of digital culture dictates that what becomes or does not become a keyword ultimately has nothing to do with semantic criteria. Even the most emotional, appellative, and antirational concept will fizzle out on Twitter if it is not preceded by a hashtag. Conversely, a trivial (and in theory even a meaningless) sequence of letters can become the most important keyword among the "trending topics" so long as it simply appears in as many tweets as possible. A notorious example of this is Donald Trump's typo "covfefe" (for "coverage"), which in May of 2017 became a hashtag that was retweeted more than 100,000 times.

Semantics, hermeneutics, meaningful content, and empathy – all central categories in historical keyword research – are utterly irrelevant to the codification process that turns a word into a hashtag. (Under the conditions of digital culture, in fact, only the last of Wülfing's six features of the keyword remains: the compulsion to repeat it.) Moreover, this fundamental difference applies just as much to the current creation of keywords as it does to their recognizability. From the beginning, linguists and historians not only associated keywords with the criterion of "emotion" but also with their ability to be identified. According to Wilhelm Bauer, who was writing nearly a century ago, "that which turns a word into a keyword – its emotional aspect – cannot be determined intellectually. . . . In the end, it can only be felt."[44] The idea that the keywords of an epoch can only be identified by extremely sensitive readers remained a constant feature in this field of linguistic research throughout the twentieth century. Beatrice Wolter, 80 years after the publication of Bauer's foundational work, would make the following remarks about the scientific process of keyword analysis: "While reading, a dialogue develops between the analyst and the corpus of texts. The high-frequency occurrence of a word will capture the attention of the investigator."[45] Regarding her methodological approach, moreover, she concludes: "With the help of certain indicators, it is possible to recognize a keyword as such, though the final decision about whether one is dealing with a keyword or not lies at the discretion of the analyst."[46]

Sensitivity, attention, discretion — these are supposed to be the core hermeneutic competencies of scientists who are attempting to identify keywords. Seven years after Wolter made these remarks, Chris Messina posted his tweet. Ever since then, the question of what a keyword is has become drastically simpler. It is no longer necessary for an "analyst" to have a sensitive "dialogue" with a body of texts. Today, a keyword is simply the # symbol and whatever letters come after it.

The hashtag thus has two forebears in the history of knowledge in the twentieth century: the keyword as a unit for organizing documents, and as a characteristic expression of a historical epoch or political agenda. The first branch of its heritage is indicative of its taxonomic function, while the second branch points to its semantic function. In the hashtag, one could say that these two genealogical strands have been brought together. On the one hand, and like a keyword in a library catalog, it serves to classify documents; on the other hand, this act of classification is no longer performed exclusively by a committee of librarians but is rather something that can be done by anyone at all on social networks, and in this case the organizational unit of the hashtag resembles the keywords or catchphrases studied by historical linguists. The hashtags #iranelection, #icebucketchallenge, and #Ferguson, for instance, are both: they are terms for cataloging an inventory of knowledge, and they are defining or characteristic concepts of their respective historical moments. The hashtag is an index and a slogan at the same time.

Yet what were the precise changes that brought about this conceptual unification? Since 2007, the Twitter hashtag has been a popular manifestation of the possibility to participate in public indexing or "keywording." Regarding the transition from the keywords of library catalogs to the hashtags of social media, however, the decisive historical shifts took place a few years earlier. They involved the media-technical conditions of a practice of indexing that was no longer restricted to specific professional milieus and accredited personnel but was rather made available to every user of the internet.

During the first half of the 1990s, when the collection of networked computer documents known as the World Wide Web was becoming increasingly unmanageable, the question was raised of how to catalog and represent this newly created archive of knowledge. Early attempts to transfer the organizational principles of large libraries to the classification of all websites – by means of a system of keywords devised by a central consortium, for instance – soon proved to be impracticable. "The internet," in the words of Isabella Peters, "grew too fast to find, consider, analyze, and allocate every website."[47] Since the mid-1990s, searching for documents on the internet has taken place almost exclusively by means of search engines, which, as every user of Google knows, do no more than provide links to complete websites arranged in a ranked list according to a cryptic system of algorithms. The idea of indexing websites by means of separate "keywords" created with greater transparency than the proprietary algorithms of corporations – an early dream of many internet activists – has remained an illusory concept on account of the ever-growing abundance of online documents.

Such was the situation of the historical threshold in digital culture that came to be known as "Web 2.0." Around the year 2004, with the widespread availability of faster broadband connections, web-enabled phones, and digital cameras, the internet began to be defined by documents and inventories of knowledge that were created and administered by users themselves. It was in this environment that the early idea of keyword-driven indexing was revived, though now no longer in the sense of a central supervisory committee (by that point, no single committee could have dealt with the expanses of the World Wide Web). Rather, such indexing could simply be done by the community of users. It was on new platforms such as Flickr or Delicious, where users could share their own websites and make comments, that archives of information first began to be organized by means of self-chosen keywords – a practice that soon came to be known as "social tagging." As is still the case today, whoever typed in a given keyword on Flickr or Delicious would receive all the photos or bookmarks that are associated with that concept on the platform in question.

It was on these websites, then, that the catalog keywords of a library's closed and centrally regulated inventory began to transform into the keywords used today to organize the open inventories of social networks, which can be expanded by anyone. What had been created, as Gene Smith noted as early as 2008, were "user-defined labels to organize and share information" and "people-powered metadata."[48] The process of indexing thus acquired a performative value. For users of Flickr or Delicious, indexing was no longer a matter of setting standards or complying with norms, but was, instead, a creative process. The poetic nature of assigning keywords, which is apparent in the best Twitter hashtags today, had its beginnings here. Since 2004, one term that has been used to designate this freely accessible form of classifying inventories of knowledge – a keyword for keywords, so to speak – is the neologism "folksonomy," which is a portmanteau of the words *folk* and *taxonomy*. Thomas Vander Wal, who claims to have invented the term, has stressed on his blog that, in the sphere of social tagging, producers and consumers are one and the same; with respect to assigning keywords, a "folksonomy" knows no external authority.[49]

Around 2004, when social tagging was developed on Flickr and Delicious, keywords could also function as a purely private classification system. It was the implementation of algorithmic operations, which connected individual keywords

45

with the posts of other users, that first allowed these archives to become "folksonomies" and that transformed social tagging into what Erika Linz has recently called "collaborative tagging."[50]

On today's social media – and this is the main difference between Delicious and Twitter, between Flickr and Instagram – this collaboration is specified in advance with the # symbol. No one who needs a keyword for private cataloging purposes would ever turn it into a hashtag. In contrast, the use of keywords on Twitter or Instagram is synonymous with the desire for accumulation, with the desire to connect one's post with others designated by the same hashtag. As regards the way that the hash sign is used today, Erika Linz's hypothesis that "the choice of a keyword is often made with a public audience in mind" is slightly off the mark.[51] It would be more accurate to say that a hashtag on Twitter or Instagram is always used to test its campaign potential. Until recently in the history of the keyword as an organizational unit, this potential played no role at all. The catalog systems of libraries do not have any "trending topics." In today's digital culture, on the contrary, the organization of statements and documents has turned the desire to "trend" into a fundamental principle of communication technology. The signature of this desire is the # symbol, whose dynamic and open-ended form embodies the hope for maximum dissemination.

5

Venues of the Hashtag I: Political Activism

When learning about the contexts in which the hashtag has played a significant role – about the scientific and professional milieus that have done the most to comprehend its functions – one will soon notice that every search on Google, through library catalogs, and in databases yields the same results. Aside from a few exceptions, reflections on the hashtag come from the same two types of sources: social-scientific and media-theoretical articles about political activism on the one hand, and insights from the world of marketing on the other. Over the past ten years, these two perspectives have overwhelmingly dominated the discussions about this new form of organizing statements, and so it should be asked what these ostensibly dissimilar contexts happen to share in common. What, if anything, unites the now familiar phenomena of using the hash sign to form both political collectives ("hashtag activism") and marketing campaigns ("hashtag marketing")?

That the # symbol is closely related to the formation of political counter-publics is already evident from the circumstances of its genesis on Twitter. Since 2005, the "Barcamp" genre of conferences, which Chris Messina used as an example in his foundational tweet, has been an open forum for discussing the issues of internet culture outside of the established conference circuit and the filtered reporting of the mass media. From its beginning, the hashtag sign was meant to bring together voices that had not been sufficiently represented by the traditional media system. This emancipatory function of the # symbol has since been stressed over and over again in studies of Twitter's role in current political movements. For instance, Axel Bruns and Jean Burgess, who in 2011 published an often-cited media-theoretical article about the use of Twitter hashtags in the creation of political resistance, underscored the "central role of the hashtag in coordinating publics."[52] In his 2012 book on social media and contemporary activism, Paolo Gerbaudo refers to the # symbol as a "means of organization, of collective action."[53] Finally, Nathan Rambukkana, whose 2015 anthology *Hashtag Publics* is the most comprehensive book on the topic to date, refers to the hashtag as "that piece of multiply repurposed typography, that rebel punctuation mark moving to establish itself in new regimes of discourse and communication."[54]

What, exactly, constitutes the rebelliousness of the hashtag? First of all, it allows individuals and groups of people who have been excluded or misrepresented by the conventional mass media to offer a visible corrective simply by pushing a few buttons on their phones or computers. "Because of the participatory nature of these activities," according to Joel Penny, "there is great potential to democratize the field of persuasive political communication that has been historically dominated by elite interests and to elevate the voices and perspectives of marginalized groups."[55] It is therefore quite consequential that the first political hashtag to last for a long time among Twitter's "trending topics" – this was during the early summer of 2009, before posts were automatically networked to others with the same keyword – came from an authoritarian country with government-censored mass media. On June 12 of that year, after President Ahmadinejad had been re-elected by "officially" two-thirds of the votes, despite a palpable mood for reform among the population, a team of authors on Twitter began, under the hashtag #iranelection, to register the collective feeling of resentment about the apparently manipulated election results, and to provide a record of the protests that were spreading through the streets of Tehran. What began with 60 tweets on that day, as an oppositional voice against the silence of the Iranian state media and the expulsion of foreign correspondents, swelled over the course of a month of escalating protests into "more than ten thousand #iranelection tweets an hour," so that, as Negar Mottahedeh has remarked, "the hashtag #iranelection remained the highest-ranking global hashtag on Twitter for two weeks following the presidential election."[56]

In social media's country of origin, too, political hashtags have become the most popular and widely distributed on Twitter, and they have likewise come to be accepted as the representative slogans of counter-movements. Under the keywords #BlackLivesMatter (since 2013) and #Ferguson (since 2014) – which have already been used more than 15 and 30 million times on Twitter, respectively[57] – statements have been formulated on the inadequate legal and journalistic treatment of two homicides involving white authority figures and unarmed black teenagers. The acquittal in July 2013 of a security guard in Florida who had shot a high-school student named Trayvon Martin, and the police killing of an 18-year-old named Michael Brown in Ferguson, Missouri, in August 2014, instigated a flurry of impressions, comments, and expressions of solidarity on Twitter that opposed the latent racism of many police forces, courts, television broadcasters, and other perspectives.

Yarimar Bonilla and Jonathan Rosa, who published a "hashtag ethnography" about the #Ferguson movement, pointed out the interesting statistic that, during the timeframe of their investigation, a significantly higher percentage of African Americans were active on Twitter than of white Americans (22 versus 16 percent).[58] The authors associate this difference with the significance of social media as a communication channel for oppositional public spheres: "It is surely not coincidental that the groups most likely . . . to be misrepresented in the media are precisely those turning to digital activism at the highest rates."[59] Moreover, regarding #Ferguson and other recent hashtags associated with protest movements, such as #HandsUpDontShoot or #IfTheyGunnedMeDown, they remark in their essay that such keywords "speak to the long history of inaccurate and unfair portrayal of African Americans within mainstream media."[60]

As these vivid passages make clear, hashtags have become the nodal points of a new media public that allows members of the population who are accustomed to being misrepresented by others to describe their own experiences directly and more truthfully, to raise their own voices without any interference from the distortive filter of the mass media, and to let out a collectively amplified #Aufschrei ("#scream"), as one popular hashtag from Germany exhorted in 2013. In social-scientific and media-theoretical research, the political power of the Twitter hashtag has often been associated with Bruno Latour's "author-network theory." According to Nathan Rambukkana, for instance, the hashtag is "an actor in its own right,"[61] and its use by online activists reinforces Latour's old idea that individuals and technologies should be regarded "as actors working to influence each other and articulate together."[62] In Negar Mottahedeh's opinion, the power of the hashtag has even resulted in the amalgamation of technologies and individuals, data and bodies. Such, at least, is a recurring argument in her book *#Iranelection*: "The Iranian postelection crisis," she writes, "galvanized and transformed the ecology of life online such that the tropes of #iranelection, its aggregation of an international mass movement around a uniform global hashtag . . . became part of a sensing, breathing, collective body, part flesh, part data."[63] Driven by the growing force of the # symbol, according to Mottahedeh, sequences of letters can be transformed into the organic bodies of protest groups.

6

Venues of the Hashtag II: Marketing

In recent years, political hashtags have tended to catch on especially well when they concern regions in which social networks can create a fundamental counter-public to the state media (in addition to #iranelection, other examples of this sort include #Tahrir from Egypt in 2011 and #BringBackOurGirls from Nigeria in 2014), or when they give a voice to groups who risk being ignored or misrepresented by the conventional media reality (#BlackLivesMatter and #Ferguson are of this type, as is #MeToo). These iconic representatives of "hashtag activism" have captured the attention of the public more than any other keywords on Twitter or Instagram.

As mentioned above, however, the brief history of the hashtag has also involved a second application or form of dissemination that has generated at least as many guidelines, commentaries, and analyses: the sphere of marketing. The connection here even has an etymological basis – "to tag" means "to mark" – and in the advanced theories of social-media-driven product communication, the hash sign now serves a central function as a catchword in advertising campaigns and slogans. Toward the end of Nathan Rambukkana's passionate argument for "activist hashtag publics," he shifts gears for a moment to discuss this second, marketing-driven use of digital indexing: "[O]ne upshot of this prominence," he remarks about the hashtag, "is, perhaps ironically, that at least in this one way, neoliberalism and activism might be speaking the same language, though obviously with different intents."[64] This brief aside, appearing as it does in one of the most powerfully written manifestos for hashtag activism to date, is rather telling (the question remains whether the category of "intent" can really play any role in explaining why these two disparate spheres of life are now "speaking the same language," but I will return to this issue below). The "rebel punctuation mark," as Rambukkana calls it, can just as well be understood as something highly sleek and manipulative, given that it focuses the attention of potential customers on particular brands, products, services, and business ideas in a manner that casually involves the community's own participation.

The hashtag is ubiquitous in today's marketing handbooks and blogs. According to one recent guide to hashtag marketing, "[H]ashtags represent an incredibly important element of digital marketing. This popular symbol has become a key driver of user engagement and an integral part of any effective social media effort."[65] Yet how, exactly, is this symbol especially suitable for expanding the reach of advertising campaigns? One could say, first of all, that a keyword affixed to a hash sign is the ideal agent of the new way of connecting with customers that has come to be known as "content marketing." Ever since digital media technology made it possible for every business to have its own website, blog, and profile on social networks – and thus to operate like a publishing house – the primary goal of "marketing" has not been to release paid advertisements for products in the mass media but rather to craft a bespoke media environment in which targeted

consumers will be guided toward particular products by means of indirect, atmospheric incentives,
such as the opportunity to join a "community" of
like-minded people. (In this regard, the Austrian
beverage company Red Bull was far ahead of
the curve; since the 1990s, its marketing depart-
ment has focused on building such communities
around the themes of sports and music.)

The hashtag enhances the effectiveness of
content marketing and its chances of success in
several respects. This is because it increases, in a
clearly marked and quantifiable manner, the level
of exchange that takes place between companies
and consumers, and among the consumers themselves. During the early years of social media, it
was admittedly possible that a company's popular
blog entry or YouTube video could make the cor-
responding link jump up the rankings in a Google
search, but such attempts at "search engine opti-
mization," which was then the ultimate goal of
all content marketing, were always tied to the
unanswerable question of whether users and
potential customers were ever really responding
to the "content" of the advertising campaign.

On Twitter and Instagram – that is, under the
conditions of the hashtag – this question is far

easier to answer. The designated keywords that companies add to their posts and pictures can be adopted by users, forwarded, and reused. They are thus an inconspicuous but effective way to increase the online presence of a brand and to create a sales-promoting community of potential customers. Companies can then track the allure of their online slogans with previously unthinkable precision, because the exact number of times that a hashtag has been clicked on or reposted on Twitter or Instagram can be calculated in an instant. In the meantime, several new companies have emerged, such as Keyhole, that provide "hashtag tracking" services for other firms by producing detailed geographical and chronological maps of a given keyword's distribution. "The use of hashtags," as one business article from 2014 put it, "connects your brand with topics that people are interested in and interacts with them through these topics. . . . Hashtags increase brand loyalty."[66] On one infographic about the benefits of using hashtags, which has been reposted on numerous marketing blogs, the following simple equation appears in large letters: "# = \$\$\$."[67] According to a post on the popular digital-marketing platform *Sprout Social*, "Consumers . . .

use the hashtag to find like-minded community members. The brand incorporates user-generated content to add authenticity to its feed." In sum: "Brand awareness is subtly spread in the hashtag."[68]

The added value that the # symbol can contribute to a marketing campaign is evident in some of the hashtags that companies have already used, such as the slogan #ShareACoke from 2012 or Kentucky Fried Chicken's #HowDoYouKFC from 2014, which prompted millions of tweets and Instagram posts and which, in the words of two critics, "was successfully converting individual social media users into positive advertisers."[69] Frequently, such hashtags are introduced as part of a promotional contest. The chain restaurant Domino's Pizza, for instance, encouraged its online followers to post with the hashtag #letsdolunch, promising reduced prices to customers whose posts surpassed a certain number.[70] American Express, in turn, started a collaboration with Twitter that involved offering cardholders gift cards for promoting certain products with specific hashtags in their tweets.[71]

This practice, however, is not categorically different from previous methods of content marketing, when slogans were disseminated by the companies themselves. Yet the hashtag does represent a novel system of brand promotion to the extent that attention can be drawn to a product by piggybacking on other popular hashtags or trending topics. This leads to the phenomenon that customers, as one marketing blogger has remarked, "might already use a branded hashtag without your knowledge."[72] In addition to coming up with their own catchy slogans, that is, companies engaged in hashtag marketing also make use of already-existing hashtags to extend the reach of their posts: "if your content relates to a topic like #beauty, #fashion, #business, or a #sale," as one columnist advises, "say so by including a hashtag." For, the author goes on, "[b]y using tags that are frequently searched, you'll greatly increase the odds that your content will appear in more hashtag searches and reach more eyes."[73]

Regarding the laws that govern the distribution of statements, this "discursive practice" (to borrow Foucault's term) is a historically new constellation. In a system of communication in which almost every post is indexed and in which these keywords are linked to one another, every word or phrase affixed to a hash sign can, with a single click, be placed into a different context, associated with a different addressee, and sent to a different audience. Internet activists consider this a dangerous practice because, as Elizabeth Losh mentions in her study of "hashtag feminism" in India, a socio-politically motivated hashtag such as #selfies4schools can suddenly be coopted, and thus parasitically undermined, by the porn industry.[74] In the world of marketing, however, this sort of repurposing is seen as an opportunity to reach new groups of customers and client bases without any extra effort. "Think of [hashtags] as search marketing keywords," recommends one piece of advice, "but with one unique feature that sets them apart. Unlike the keywords in your paid search campaign – most of which are built around highly specific, less common terms – most of the hashtags you use should already be popular and known to an audience."[75]

By clustering tweets and Instagram posts together, the # symbol makes their statements generally exchangeable. Every post labeled with the same hashtag – regardless of its intended content or its original context – is placed into a networked relationship with all the others. From the perspective of marketing, this situation is ideal because a sequence of letters and a hash sign are all that is needed to tap into a glamorous region of Twitter or Instagram, to reach the top position among the trending topics of the day, and thus to profit from this visibility. The hashtag therefore makes it possible for companies to transform words and phrases from any given context into advertising mechanisms for their own products. Strictly speaking, the hashtag bestows upon words the form of a commodity. The hash sign endows the designated sequence of letters with an exchange value without, however, associating it with any specific meaning or unique property. In this light, the rebellious nature that Nathan Rambukkana would like to attribute to the hashtag is far less prominent than its unifying or equalizing function.

One could say that the hashtag commodifies the words that follow it. In the famous chapter on reification in his 1923 book *History and Class Consciousness*, Georg Lukács hoped to demonstrate "the extent to which ... exchange is the dominant form of metabolic change in a society."[76] This diagnosis applies perfectly to the metabolism of social media one century later. In Lukács's analysis of the processes of reification, the two most significant categories in the commodity system are those of "levelling" and "exchangeability." To make this case, he cites Marx's fundamental hypothesis that products "assume the form of commodities inasmuch as they are exchangeables, i.e., expressions of one and the same third."[77] "The commodity form," according to Lukács, "facilitates the equal exchange of qualitatively different objects."[78] In the hashtag, this act of exchanging and leveling takes place in the realm of language. Non-catalogable, unique, and intractable elements are irrelevant in its logic. What matters instead is the greatest possible accumulation of posts, the accumulation of uniform and identically hashtagged capital (in the form of statements), which can be represented in quantifiable lists (such as Twitter's "trending topics") and is expected to keep on growing.

With this background in mind, it is interesting to note that a complex debate has been taking place in recent years over the question of whether hashtags can be registered as trademarks. Since 2010, around 5,000 trademark applications have been filed for hashtags, above all at the Patent and Trademark Office in the United States.[79] As a strategy, it has become more common for companies to seek protection for hashtags such as #smilewithacoke, #HowDoYouKFC, or #sayitwithpepsi (three examples of registered trademarks) and to control the circulation of these commodified words on social media. Led by marketing theorists and patent lawyers, the controversial discussions have made it clear, however, that the way in which hashtags are used requires a more nuanced perspective in comparison to brand names or advertising slogans.

In the few rulings and studies that have addressed this legal issue, most judges and commentators have taken the position that "hashtags may never be protectable as trademarks."[80] According to the legal scholar Robert Sherwin, this is because they are "a tool that encourages use by others."[81] Trademark law in the United States permits words or slogans to be protected only when they have a clear "source identifier, which does not apply in the case of hashtags because they are used freely and diffusely. Consumer confusion about the source of a brand name, which is normally protected by trademark law, plays no role in the circulation of hashtags."[82]

In cases where the Patent and Trademark Office has accepted a given hashtag as a registered trademark, as in the 2013 ruling in favor of protecting #HowDoYouKFC, the decisions were based explicitly on the fact that the corporations in question had been using the hashtag mark in a "non-internet context." "In each of these cases," as David Kohane has summarized, "the PTO concluded that the specimen submitted in support of the registration application evidenced use of the hashtag mark as a trademark, not merely as a means of facilitating on-line search. Each specimen prominently displayed the hashtag mark . . . on endcaps or signage."[83]

The opinion of marketing specialists on trademarking hashtags has basically been ambivalent. On the one hand, the great success of advertising campaigns such as #ShareACoke or #HowDoYouKFC can "encourage corporations to seek trademark protection for hashtags to protect exclusive use," as Kendall Salter has remarked in what remains the most detailed legal study of the issue.[84] On the other hand, hashtags "allow users to proliferate the mark through widespread use in social media platforms. . . . The essence of a hashtag is user interaction."[85] This may result in companies losing some control over their marketing strategies, but the uncontrolled spread of their hashtags on social media represents even greater marketing power for the products being advertised.

The idea of trademarking viral hashtags is so attractive, in fact, that even popular keywords from the realm of internet activism have been the subject of trademark debates. In July 2014, for instance, an asthmatic man was choked to death by a police officer in New York, and this event instigated the hashtag #Icantbreathe on Twitter. Shortly thereafter, two companies tried to trademark it. The hashtag #JeSuisCharlie, which was created as a token of solidarity after the magazine *Charlie Hebdo*'s editorial office had been attacked in Paris, inspired, in France alone, "more than 50 separate applications to register the phrase as a trademark, none of which came from the actual creator of the original image and words."[86] Regardless of the fact that all of these applications were rejected at the time, the impulse of agencies and companies to try to trademark these examples as well undoubtedly has something to do with the particular form of commodity that hashtagged statements have come to represent.

It seems to make little difference whether they happen to refer to a product or a social movement, to a service or a person's death, so long as the scent of profit is in the air. In the words of a German social-media consultant: "As #scream [#Aufschrei] has demonstrated all too clearly, the hashtag is an ideal framework for clustering topics together, topics that can pertain just as well to products or to PR."[87]

Among the several hashtags that have been trademarked in recent years, there is one that demonstrates their effects in an especially vivid manner. Before the 2016 Olympic Games in Rio de Janeiro, the United States Olympic Committee (USOC) stipulated that the hashtag #Rio2016 could only be used by the event's main sponsors, which included the likes of Coca-Cola, McDonald's, Visa, and Samsung. Every athlete representing the United States received a letter from the USOC prohibiting their sponsors and marketing affiliates from using this hashtag in tweets and Instagram posts. When interviewed about this gesture, an intellectual property lawyer named Mark Terry offered the following critical response: "Trademark infringement occurs when another party uses a trademark and confuses the public as to the source of a product or service that's being used in commerce. That's not what happens when you use a hashtag. I'm not selling a product or service, I'm just making statements on an open forum. How else do you indicate you are talking about the 2016 Olympics without saying #Rio2016?"[88] This last sentence, above all, is indicative of the changes that the emergence of the hashtag has entailed for the dispersion of statements. For it raises questions about the status of words: Are they a means of communication or a particular form of commodity, protected trademarks or elements of freely circulating discourse? The hashtag has unquestionably blurred these boundaries.

7

Empowering and Leveling

During the short decade in which the hashtag has operated as a coordinator of statements and documents, its main areas of application have thus been heterogeneous, and seem – at least at first glance – to have little in common. As a signature of oppositional social and political movements – #Ferguson, #BlackLivesMatter, and #MeToo are just three of many examples – it has undoubtedly been responsible for giving a loud and collective voice to previously ignored groups of people, and for bringing previously overlooked concerns to the attention of the public sphere. At the same time, however, the hashtag's prominent role in contemporary marketing demonstrates that its profit-oriented application is not only central but also inherent in the way that it turns statements into entities that can be exchanged and accumulated. As Chris Messina has stressed, the # symbol *labels* that which is expressed and shared; it thus makes dispersed statements visible, but it couples this new visibility with an act of registration and leveling.

One way in which the hashtag can be used opposes this trend. Here I have in mind those hashtags that, rather than referring to a popular slogan or concept, are meant to supplement their own tweets or Instagram posts in a singular and idiosyncratic way. This sort of hashtag, as Julia Turner has pointed out, "gives the writer the opportunity to comment on his own emotional state, to sarcastically undercut his own tweet, to construct an extra layer of irony, to offer a flash of evocative imagery or to deliver metaphors with striking economy."[89] In this form, the hashtag resists the demand for accumulation and instead remains part of a closed textual unit within which it can generate ironic or poetic effects. This playful application undermines the functions dictated by its media default settings.

The ironic and self-reflective use of the keyword has no place, however, in hashtag activism or hashtag marketing. Both spheres are instead concerned with the uniformity of statements that are labeled with the same hashtag; here, the # symbol is meant to transform – even in the sphere of internet activism – the posts subsumed under it into brand ambassadors. Even the initiators of the Occupy Wall Street movement were aware of the hashtag's advertising appeal. In July 2011, a website called Adbusters used the motto #OccupyWallStreet as an invitation for protesters to gather in Zuccotti Park. "The very name of the campaign," as Paolo Gerbaudo remarked about the movement, "was turned into a hashtag . . . so as to facilitate its 'viral' diffusion."[90] In 2011, however, this was not (yet) a proven tactic. Throughout that summer, in fact, "the #OccupyWallStreet hashtag never got close to becoming a trending topic,"[91] and it was not until protesters physically occupied Zuccotti Park that the catchphrase began to resonate on social media. Even though the strategy initially fell flat, #OccupyWallStreet was probably the first political hashtag in the United States to be developed explicitly for marketing reasons. It was, in other words, the first activist hashtag logo.

What, exactly, does Nathan Rambukkana mean when he says that, with the hashtag, "neoliberalism and activism might be speaking the same language, though obviously with different intents"?[92] In the desire to bring about socio-political change or promote products, does the factor of "intent" even matter anymore, now that both types of campaign have begun to use the same methods? It is telling that the techniques of self-marketing now regularly play a role in hashtag activism, of all things. Of course, this trend has seeped into other areas of life as well. In the anthology edited by Rambukkana, for instance, there is an essay about digital self-representations in higher education that considers the ways in which "hashtags on Twitter contribute to building and maintaining academic identity, such as promoting one's own work by using hashtags."[93] In a section of the essay with the subtitle "#IDENTITY," the author adds: "Creating an online presence or brand becomes almost as important as building a robust CV. . . . Hashtags have become important identity units, and creating the right combination of units has become important for careers and connections."[94]

Under the conditions of digital culture, there is now a patently stronger connection between political engagement and strategies for self-promotion. Today, the struggles against racial and sexual discrimination or economic inequality are in harmony with methods of self-representation, which draw from the techniques and vocabulary of marketing. This is a surprising alliance, given that those who are critical of economic injustice and social marginalization tend to frown upon self-commodification as well. Yet this is seldom the case in the field of hashtag activism, as the passages quoted above make abundantly clear, and perhaps this is because the ugly face of "neoliberalism," on which Rambukkana shines a brief light in his argument on behalf of the "rebel punctuation mark," is simply an inherent feature of the hashtag and its inexhaustible use. Day after day, one can witness on Instagram how a few professional (and countless self-proclaimed) "influencers" blur the line between their private lives and marketing campaigns. One can see, too, how the right hashtag will increase the popularity of their posts, boost the symbolic capital of their profiles, and even cause real money to flow into their bank accounts. As it seems to me, no political critique of the present day would be complete without taking into account these processes of collective commodification, and analyzing how the hashtag-driven compulsion to accumulate affects both products and people, services and activism.

The dilemma of the hashtag – the fact that it empowers people yet also places everything on the same level – became especially apparent in the events surrounding the #MeToo movement. This debate began in the fall of 2017 and has since transformed cultural attitudes toward sexual harassment and violence in a way that can perhaps only be compared to the historical upheavals of 1968. Instigated by two magazine articles about the film producer Harvey Weinstein and by the actress Alyssa Milano's famous tweet from October 15, 2017 ("If you've been sexually harassed or assaulted write 'me too' as a reply to this tweet"),[95] it has without a doubt increased society's collective sensitivity toward forms of sexualized violence and its awareness of the connections between power relations and sexual harassment.

What has also been remarkable over the course of the debate are the numerous conflicts and controversies about how "sexualized violence" should be understood, and what specific violations are deserving of the hashtag #MeToo. During the winter months of 2017 and 2018, hardly a day passed without someone raising the question, either on social media or in the traditional media, about where the boundary lies between legitimate intimacy and illegitimate harassment. One hotly discussed and debated example of this was the open letter signed by 100 well-known women in France – the signatories included the likes of Catherine Deneuve and Catherine Millet – which states: "Rape is a crime, but insistent or clumsy flirting is not an offense, nor is gallantry macho aggression."[96]

The opinions expressed in this letter about what constitutes sexual transgression elicited a great deal of both criticism and approval, all of which has been discussed elsewhere at length. For the purposes of this book, it is necessary to ask whether the hashtag, as a medium and catalyst of the debate, has contributed to the problems associated with drawing clear boundaries. If its function as a distributor of statements is taken seriously, then it must be said that its compulsion to subsume things and make them uniform undoubtedly has the effect of blurring boundaries and leveling out that which is unique and incommensurable. In order to participate in this debate, every contributor had to post her individual experiences, stories, and opinions under the same keyword. Without the rubricating power of the hashtag, any post in support of the #MeToo movement would immediately fade into oblivion, both for technical reasons and because of its "insufficient" content. This media condition, however, has only increased the very dangers of homogenization and unclear boundaries that have so often been criticized over the course of the debate.

A good decade after its appearance, the hashtag is thus characterized by its irresolvable ambivalence. It allows scattered voices to be heard while simultaneously suppressing their unique and nonexchangeable qualities.

Notes

1 Theodor W. Adorno, "Punctuation Marks," trans. Shierry Weber Nicholsen, *The Antioch Review* 48 (1990), 300–5, at 300.
2 Quoted from https://twitter.com/chrismessina/status/223115412?lang=de.
3 Chris Messina, "Groups for Twitter; or A Proposal for Twitter Tag Channels," *Factory Joe* (August 25, 2007), https://factoryjoe.com/2007/08/25/groups-for-twitter-or-a-proposal-for-twitter-tag-channels (emphasis original).
4 Axel Bruns and Jean Burgess, "Twitter Hashtags from Ad Hoc to Calculated Publics," in *Hashtag Publics: The Power and Politics of Discursive Networks*, ed. Nathan Rambukkana (New York: Peter Lang, 2015), 13–28, at 18.
5 Quoted from Lexi Pandell, "An Oral History

of the #Hashtag," *Wired* (May 19, 2017), www. wired.com/2017/05/oral-history-hashtag.

6 Quoted from https://twitter.com/lmorchard/ statuses/218773732.

7 See Leslie Michael Orchard, "Sticky Tags for Twitter?" *oxDECAFBAD* (August 22, 2007), https://decafbad.com/blog/2007/08/22/sticky-tags-for-twitter.

8 On Twitter's Track function, see https://blog. twitter.com/official/en_us/a/2007/tracking-twitter.html.

9 Quoted from Pandell, "An Oral History of the #Hashtag," n.p.

10 Quoted from ibid.

11 Michel Foucault, *The Archaeology of Knowledge & The Discourse on Language*, trans. A. M. Sheridan Smith (New York: Pantheon Books, 1972), 28.

12 Ibid., 31, 99.

13 Ibid., 37.

14 Ibid., 92.

15 Paola-Maria Caleffi, "The 'Hashtag': A New Word or a New Rule?" *SKASE Journal of Theoretical Linguistics* 12 (2015), 46–69, at 48, 67.

16 See the many examples cited by Thomas A. Fine, "The Sign of the Number," *Sentence Spacing: A Typographic Counter-Revolution* (October 6,

2015), http://widespacer.blogspot.com/2015/10/the-sign-of-number.html.

17 Keith Houston, *Shady Characters: The Secret Life of Punctuation, Symbols, and Other Typographical Marks* (New York: W. W. Norton, 2013), 42.

18 For an image of the abbreviation written in Newton's hand, see Fine, "The Sign of the Number," n.p.

19 On the Toronto conference and the development of the universal keyboard in general, see Ernst Martin, *Die Schreibmaschine und ihre Entwicklungsgeschichte* (Aachen: Basten, 1949; repr. 2003), 548, 531 (where there is also an illustration of the Remington 2 keyboard).

20 Douglas Kerr, "The ASCII Character 'Octatherp,'" *The Pumpkin* (May 8, 2006), http://dougkerr.net/Pumpkin/articles/Octatherp.pdf.

21 For a technical description of this process, see Douglas Kerr, "The Names 'Octatherp' and 'Octotherp' for the Symbol '#,'" *The Pumpkin* (December 8, 2014), http://dougkerr.net/Pumpkin/articles/Octatherp-octotherp.pdf, 2, 4.

22 Ibid.

23 See Kerr, "The Names 'Octatherp' and 'Octotherp,'" 7; and Houston, *Shady Characters*, 49.

24 Jeff Scheible, *Digital Shift: The Cultural Logic of Punctuation* (Minneapolis: University of Minnesota Press, 2015), 119. For Scheible's entire discussion of the role of the hash sign on touchtone telephones, see pages 118–22 of his book.

25 Christian Kämmerling, "Nimm es in Gottes Namen," *Die Weltwoche* (August 27, 2003), weltwoche.ch/ausgaben/2003_35/artikel/nimm-es-in-gottes-namen-die-weltwoche-ausgabe-352 003.html.

26 See Charles Cutter, *Rules of a Printer Dictionary Catalogue* (Washington, DC: Public Printing Office, 1904); and Frauke Bartelt, *Standardlisten zur Schlagwortgebung: Hilfsmittel der verbalen Sacherschließung in Bibliotheken* (Cologne: Greven, 1978), 15–16.

27 Heinrich Roloff, *Lehrbuch der Sachkatalogisierung*, 3rd edn. (Munich: Verlag Dokumentation, 1968), 31 [translated – hereafter "trans."].

28 Quoted from Franz Förschner, *Eine Theorie zum Schlagwortkatalog* (Wiesbaden: Harrassowitz, 1987), 5 [trans.]. On the debates in the field of library science during the first third of the twentieth century, see Martin Heinrici, *Der Bibliothekar als Betrüger: Schlagwort und Aufstellung – Schlagwortkatalog und Standortkatalog* (Vienna:

Zell-Verlag, 1931); and Karl-Heinz Spieler, *Zur Theorie des Schlagwortkatalogs* (Berlin: Deutscher Bibliotheksverband, 1975).

29 Roloff, *Lehrbuch der Sachkatalogisierung*, 115 [trans.].

30 Agnes Stählin, "Kleine Sprachlehre des Schlagwortkatalogs," in *Festschrift Eugen Stollreither zum 75. Geburtstage gewidmet von Fachgenossen, Schülern, Freunden*, ed. Fritz Redenbacher (Erlangen: Universitätsbibliothek, 1950), 333–44, at 333 [trans.].

31 For the guidelines of the catalog of Zurich's municipal library, for instance, see Wilhelm von Wyss, *Über den Schlagwortkatalog: Mit Regeln für die Stadtbibliothek Zürich* (Zurich: Stadtbibliothek, 1909); and for those of the catalog used at the University of Erlangen's library, see Agnes Stählin and Roswitha Poll, *Regeln für den Schlagwortkatalog "Erlanger Regelwerk"* (Munich: Verlag Dokumentation, 1977).

32 Roloff, *Lehrbuch der Sachkatalogisierung*, 121 [trans.].

33 For the current edition of these rules, visit the German National Library's website at https://d-nb.info/1126513032/34.

34 On the "Subject Headings Authority File," the

name of which has since been changed to the "Gemeinsame Normdatei" ("Integrated Authority File"), see dnb.de/DE/Standardisierung/GND/gnd_node.html.

35 See help.twitter.com/en/using-twitter/how-to-use-hashtags.

36 See, for instance, Mark Dang-Anh et al., "Kontextualisierung durch Hashtags: Die Mediatisierung des politischen Sprachgebrauchs im Internet," in *Öffentliche Wörter: Analysen zum öffentlich-medialen Sprachgebrauch,* ed. Hans-Joachim Diekmannshenke and Thomas Niehr (Stuttgart: Ibidem-Verlag, 2013), 137–59, at 142; and Michele Zappavigna, "Searchable Talk: The Linguistic Functions of Hashtags," *Social Semiotics* 25 (2015), 274–91, at 277.

37 Roloff, *Lehrbuch der Sachkatalogisierung,* 115 [trans.].

38 Jeff Huang et al., "Conversational Tagging in Twitter," in *HT '10: Proceedings of the 21st ACM Conference on Hypertext and Hypermedia* (New York: ACM, 2010), 173–8, at 173.

39 Friedrich Lepp, *Schlagwörter des Reformations-zeitalter* (Leipzig: Heinsius, 1908), 1 [trans.].

40 Wilhelm Bauer, "Das Schlagwort als sozialpsy-chische und geistesgeschichtliche Erscheinung,"

Historische Zeitschrift 122 (1920), 189–240, at 208, 212 [trans.]. Wilhelm Bauer's enthusiasm for keyword-driven politics did not remain a matter of mere theory. He went on to support the National-Socialist leanings of the University of Vienna, where he belonged to an anti-Semitic group of professors known as the *Bärenhöhle* (Bear Cave). As early as the 1920s, the latter group tried to prevent Jewish professors from being hired by the university.

41 Wulf Wülfing, *Schlagworte des Jungen Deutschland: Mit einer Einführung in die Schlagwortforschung* (Berlin: Erich Schmidt, 1982), 38–40.

42 Beatrice Wolter, *Deutsche Schlagwörter zur Zeit des Dreßigjährigen Krieges* (Frankfurt am Main: Peter Lang, 2000), 23 [trans.].

43 Bauer, "Das Schlagwort," 231.

44 Ibid., 238.

45 Wolter, *Deutsche Schlagwörter*, 21.

46 Ibid., 39.

47 Isabella Peters, *Folksonomies: Indexing and Retrieval in Web 2.0* (Berlin: De Gruyter, 2009), 129.

48 Gene Smith, *Tagging: People-Powered Metadata for the Social Web* (Berkeley: New Riders, 2008), vii.

49 See http://vanderwal.net/folksonomy.html.

50 See Erika Linz, "Kollaboratives Tagging," in *Kollaboration: Beiträge zur Medientheorie und Kulturgeschichte der Zusammenarbeit*, ed. Nacim Ghanbari et al. (Paderborn: Wilhelm Fink, 2018), 83–95, esp. 84–9 [trans.].

51 Ibid., 92 [trans.].

52 Bruns and Burgess, "Twitter Hashtags from Ad Hoc to Calculated Publics," 13.

53 Paolo Gerbaudo, *Tweets and the Streets: Social Media and Contemporary Activism* (London: Pluto Press, 2012), 3.

54 Nathan Rambukkana, "From #RaceFail to #Ferguson: The Digital Intimacies of Race-Activist Hashtag Publics," in *Hashtag Publics: The Power and Politics of Discursive Networks*, ed. Rambukkana (New York: Peter Lang, 2015), 29–46, at 29.

55 Joel Penny, *The Citizen Marketer: Promoting Political Opinion in the Social Media Age* (New York: Oxford University Press, 2017), 7. See also Anne Antonakis-Nashif, "Hashtagging the Invisible: Bringing Private Experiences into Public Debate," in *Hashtag Publics: The Power and Politics of Discursive Networks*, ed. Nathan Rambukkana (New York: Peter Lang, 2015),

101–13, at 101: "the specific communicative dispositions of hashtags have opened up new possibilities for political participation and contestation to those who feel underrepresented in traditional media public."

56 Negar Mottahedeh, *#Iranelection: Hashtag Solidarity and the Transformation of Online Life* (Stanford University Press, 2015), 7. See also Michele Zappavigna, *Discourse of Twitter and Social Media: How We Use Language to Create Affiliation on the Web* (London: Sydney Bloomsbury, 2015), 174: "[#iranelection] became the first prevalent political hashtag to be reported in news media."

57 For these numbers, see Wesley Lowery, "Black Lives Matter: Birth of a Movement," *The Guardian* (January 17, 2017), www.theguardian. com / us - news / 2017 / jan / 17 / black - lives - matter - birth-of-a-movement.

58 Yarimar Bonilla and Jonathan Rosa, "#Ferguson: Digital Protest, Hashtag Ethnography, and the Racial Politics of Social Media in the United States," *American Ethnologist* 42 (2015), 4–17, at 6.

59 Ibid., 8.

60 Ibid., 9.

61 Nathan Rambukkana, "#Introduction: Hashtags

as Technosocial Events," in *Hashtag Publics: The Power and Politics of Discursive Networks*, ed. Rambukkana (New York: Peter Lang, 2015), 1–10, at 5.

62 Ibid., 4.

63 Mottahedeh, *#Iranelection*, 8. For similar passages in her book about the transformation of data into bodies, see pages 17–18 and 103 4.

64 Rambukkana, "From #RaceFail to #Ferguson," 42.

65 Pamela Nichols, "Hashtag Marketing: How to Use Hashtags that Fit Your Brand," *Blue Fountain Media* (October 1, 2017), www.bluefountain media.com/blog/hashtag-marketing-for-your-brand See also Sebastian Merz's self-published brochure *#Hashtag-Marketing: How You Can Find Readers and Customers with Hashtag Marketing* (Berlin: Sebastian Merz, 2015), which is advertised as follows: "The expert knows: If you want to achieve a higher ranking in search engines and get ahead of the global internet market, you will not get around strategic hashtag marketing." This blurb is quoted from www.amazon.de/Hashtag-Marketing-read ers-customers-hashtag-marketing-ebook/dp/B01 48D7JDA.

66 Shea Bennett, "The History of the Hashtag in Social Media Marketing," *Adweek* (September 2, 2014), www.adweek.com/digital/history-hashtag-social-marketing.

67 See, for instance, http://digitalmarketingphilippines.com/the-history-and-power-of-hashtags-in-social-media-marketing-infographic.

68 Jenn Chen, "How to Use Hashtag Marketing to Dramatically Boost Brand Awareness," *Sprout Social* (February 13, 2018), https://sproutsocial.com/insights/hashtag-marketing.

69 Linnea Laestadius and Megan Wahl, "Mobilizing Social Media Users to Become Advertisers: Corporate Hashtag Campaigns as a Public Health Concern," *Digital Health* 3 (2017), 1–12, at 7.

70 See Todd Wasserman, "Six Successful Twitter Hashtag Campaigns," *Mashable* (March 23, 2012), https://mashable.com/2012/03/23/twitter-hashtag-campaigns.

71 See Heather Kelly, "Twitter and Amex to Let You Pay with a Hashtag," *CNN: International Edition* (February 12, 2013), https://edition.cnn.com/2013/02/11/tech/social-media/twitter-hashtag-purchases.

72 Chen, "How to Use Hashtag Marketing," n.p.

73 Nichols, "Hashtag Marketing," n.p.

74 Elizabeth Losh, "Hashtag Feminism and Twitter Activism in India," *Social Epistemology Review and Reply* 3 (2014), 11–22, at 16.

75 Nichols, "Hashtag Marketing," n.p.

76 Georg Lukács, *History and Class Consciousness: Studies in Marxist Dialectics*, trans. Rodney Livingstone (Cambridge, MA: MIT Press, 1971), 84.

77 Ibid., 85.

78 Ibid., 87. For an additional analysis of commodities that focuses on aspects of standardization and leveling, see Alfred Sohn-Rethel, *Warenform und Denkform* (Frankfurt am Main: Suhrkamp, 1978), 103–33.

79 For these figures, see Kendall Salter, "The Trouble with Tags: Seeking Mark Protection for Corporate Branded Hashtags – More Trouble than It's Worth," *Journal of Corporation Law* 43 (2018), 699–713, at 701.

80 David Kohane, "#UNDECIDED: Trademark Protection for Hashtags," *IPWatchdog* (June 24, 2016), www.ipwatchdog.com/2016/06/24/undecided-trademark-protection-hashtags/id=70111.

81 Quoted from Salter, "The Trouble with Tags," 705.

82 See Elizabeth A. Falconer, "#CanHashtagsBe Trademarked: Trademark Law and the Development of Hashtags," *North Carolina Journal of Law & Technology* 17 (2016), 1–42, at 3.

83 Kohane, "#UNDECIDED," n.p.

84 Salter, "The Trouble with Tags," 707.

85 Ibid.

86 Claire Jones, "What Can You #Trademark?" *Norfolk Chamber of Commerce* (2018), norfolk-chamber.co.uk/blog/member/marketing-pr/what-can-you-trademark.

87 Josef Rankl, "Hashtag Marketing," *EMarCon* (September 16, 2013), https://emarcon.de/hashtag-marketing [trans.].

88 Quoted from Olivia Solon, "US Olympic Committee Bullying Unofficial Sponsors Who Use Hashtags," *The Guardian* (July 22, 2016), www.theguardian.com/sport/2016/jul/22/us-olympic-committee-bullying-unofficial-sponsors-hashtags.

89 Julia Turner, "#InPraiseOfTheHashtag," *New York Times Magazine* (November 2, 2012), www.nytimes.com/2012/11/04/magazine/in-praise-of-the-hashtag.html.

90 Gerbaudo, *Tweets and the Streets*, 110.

91 Ibid., 116.

92 Rambukkana, "From #RaceFail to #Ferguson," 42.

93 Sava Saheli Singh, "Hashtagging #HigherEd," in *Hashtag Publics: The Power and Politics of Discursive Networks*, ed. Nathan Rambukkana (New York: Peter Lang, 2015), 267–72, at 267.

94 Ibid., 272.

95 Quoted from https://twitter.com/alyssa_milano/status/919659438700670976?lang=en.

96 Quoted from Frank Andrews et al., "Catherine Deneuve Denounces #MeToo in Open Letter," *CNN: U.S. Edition* (January 11, 2018), www.cnn.com/2018/01/10/europe/catherine-deneuve-france-letter-metoo-intl/index.html.

Bibliography

Adorno, Theodor W. "Punctuation Marks." Trans. Shierry Weber Nicholsen. *The Antioch Review* 48 (1990): 300–5.

Andrews, Frank, et al. "Catherine Deneuve Denounces #MeToo in Open Letter." *CNN: U.S. Edition* (January 11, 2018): www.cnn.com/2018/01/10/ europe / catherine - deneuve - france - letter - metoo - intl/index.html.

Antonakis-Nashif, Anne. "Hashtagging the Invisible: Bringing Private Experiences into Public Debate." In *Hashtag Publics: The Power and Politics of Discursive Networks*. Ed. Nathan Rambukkana. New York: Peter Lang, 2015, 101–13.

Bartelt, Frauke. *Standardlisten zur Schlagwortgebung: Hilfsmittel der verbalen Sacherschliessung in Bibliotheken*. Cologne: Greven, 1978.

Bauer, Wilhelm. "Das Schlagwort als sozialpsychische und geistesgeschichtliche Erscheinung." *Historische Zeitschrift* 122 (1920): 189–240.

Bennett, Shea. "The History of the Hashtag in Social Media Marketing." *Adweek* (September 2, 2014): www.adweek.com/digital/history-hashtag-social-marketing.

Bonilla, Yarimar, and Jonathan Rosa. "#Ferguson: Digital Protest, Hashtag Ethnography, and the Racial Politics of Social Media in the United States." *American Ethnologist* 42 (2015): 4–17.

Bourdieu, Pierre. "The Economics of Linguistic Exchanges." *Social Science Information* 16 (1977): 545–668.

Bruns, Axel, and Jean Burgess. "Twitter Hashtags from Ad Hoc to Calculated Publics." In *Hashtag Publics: The Power and Politics of Discursive Networks*. Ed. Nathan Rambukkana. New York: Peter Lang, 2015, 13–28.

Caleffi, Paola-Maria. "The 'Hashtag': A New Word or a New Rule?" *SKASE Journal of Theoretical Linguistics* 12 (2015): 46–69.

Chen, Jenn. "How to Use Hashtag Marketing to Dramatically Boost Brand Awareness." *Sprout Social* (February 13, 2018): https://sproutsocial.com/insights/hashtag-marketing.

Clark, Rosemary, "'Hope in a Hashtag': The Discursive Activism of #WhyIStayed." *Feminist Media Studies* 16 (2016): 788–804.

Cunha, E., G. Magno, G. Comarela, V. Almeida, M. A. Gonçalves, and F. Benevenuto, "Analyzing the Dynamic Evolution of Hashtags on Twitter: A Language-based Approach." *Proceedings of the Workshop on Language in Social Media* (LSM 2011), Stroudsberg, PA: ACL, 58–65.

Cutter, Charles. *Rules of a Printer Dictionary Catalogue.* Washington, DC: Public Printing Office, 1904.

Dang-Anh, Mark, et al. "Kontextualisierung durch Hashtags: Die Mediatisierung des politischen Sprachgebrauchs im Internet." In *Öffentliche Wörter: Analysen zum öffentlich-medialen Sprachgebrauch.* Ed. Hans-Joachim Diekmannshenke and Thomas Niehr. Stuttgart: Ibidem-Verlag, 2013, 137–59.

Dingwerth, Leonhard. *Historische Schreibmaschinen: Faszination der alten Technik – Ein Ratgeber für Sammler und Leitfaden für Interessenten.* Delbrück: Verlag Dingwerth, 1993.

Falconer, Elizabeth A. "#CanHashtagsBeTrademarked: Trademark Law and the Development of Hashtags." *North Carolina Journal of Law & Technology* 17 (2016): 1–42.

Fine, Thomas A. "The Sign of the Number." *Sentence Spacing: A Typographic Counter-Revolution* (October 6, 2015): http://widespacer.blogspot.com/2015/10/the-sign-of-number.html.

Foucault, Michel. *The Archaeology of Knowledge & The Discourse on Language*. Trans. A. M. Sheridan Smith. New York: Pantheon Books, 1972.

Förschner, Franz. *Eine Theorie zum Schlagwortkatalog*. Wiesbaden: Harrassowitz, 1987.

French Strout, Ruth, "The Development of the Catalog and Cataloging Codes." *The Library Quarterly* 26 (1956): 254–75.

Gerbaudo, Paolo. *Tweets and the Streets: Social Media and Contemporary Activism*. London: Pluto Press, 2012.

Giglietto, Fabio, and Yenn Lee, "A Hashtag Worth a Thousand Words: Discursive Strategies Around #JeNeSuisPasCharlie After the 2015 Charlie Hebdo Shooting." *Social Media & Society* 3 (2017): 1–15.

Glanz, Berit. "Rhetorik des Hashtags." *Pop-Zeitschrift* (September 18, 2018): www.pop-zeitschrift.de/2018/09/18/social-media-september-von-berit-glanz.

Heinrici, Martin. *Der Bibliothekar als Betrüger: Schlagwort und Aufstellung – Schlagwortkatalog und Standortkatalog*. Vienna: Zell-Verlag, 1931.

Houston, Keith. *Shady Characters: The Secret Life of Punctuation, Symbols, and Other Typographical Marks*. New York: W. W. Norton, 2013.

Huang, Jeff, et al. "Conversational Tagging in Twitter." In *HT '10: Proceedings of the 21st ACM Conference on Hypertext and Hypermedia*. New York: ACM, 2010, 173–8.

Illouz, Eva (ed.). *Emotions as Commodities: Capitalism, Consumption and Authenticity*. Routledge Studies in the Sociology of Emotions. London: Routledge, 2017.

Jones, Claire. "What Can You #Trademark?" *Norfolk Chamber of Commerce* (2018): norfolk chamber.co.uk/blog/member/marketing-pr/what-can-you-trademark.

Kämmerling, Christian. "Nimm es in Gottes Namen." *Die Weltwoche* (August 27, 2003): weltwoche. ch/ausgaben/2003_35/artikel/nimm-es-in-gottes-namen-die-weltwoche-ausgabe-352003.html.

Kelly, Heather. "Twitter and Amex to Let You Pay with a Hashtag." *CNN: International Edition* (February 12, 2013): https://edition.cnn.com/2013/02/11/tech/social-media/twitter-hashtag-purchases.

Kerr, Douglas. "The ASCII Character 'Octatherp.'" *The Pumpkin* (May 8, 2006): dougkerr.net/Pumpkin/articles/Octatherp.pdf.

Kerr, Douglas. "The Names 'Octatherp' and 'Octo-therp' for the Symbol '#.'" *The Pumpkin* (December 8, 2014): http://dougkerr.net/Pumpkin/articles/Octatherp-octotherp.pdf.

Kohane, David. "#UNDECIDED: Trademark Protection for Hashtags." *IPWatchdog* (June 24, 2016): www.ipwatchdog.com/2016/06/24/undecided-trademark-protection-hashtags/id-70111.

Laestadius, Linnea, and Megan Wahl. "Mobilizing Social Media Users to Become Advertisers: Corporate Hashtag Campaigns as a Public Health Concern." *Digital Health* 3 (2017): 1–12.

Lepp, Friedrich. *Schlagwörter des Reformationszeitalter.* Leipzig: Heinsius, 1908.

Lin, Y., D. Margolin, B. Keegan, A. Baronchelli, and D. Lazer. "# Bigbirds Never Die: Understanding Social Dynamics of Emergent Hashtag." *Proceedings of the 7th International AAAI Conference on Weblogs and Social Media* (July 8–11, 2013): www.aaai.org/ocs/index.php/ICWSM/ICWSM13/paper/view/6083/6376.

Linz, Erika. "Kollaboratives Tagging." In *Kollaboration: Beiträge zur Medientheorie und Kulturgeschichte der Zusammenarbeit.* Ed. Nacim Ghanbari et al. Paderborn: Wilhelm Fink, 2018, 83–95.

Losh, Elizabeth. "Hashtag Feminism and Twitter Activism in India." *Social Epistemology Review and Reply* 3 (2014): 11–22.

Lowery, Wesley. "Black Lives Matter: Birth of a Movement." *The Guardian* (January 17, 2017): www. theguardian.com/us-news/2017/jan/17/black-lives-matter-birth-of-a-movement.

Ma, Zongyang, Aixis Sun, and Gao Cong. "Will This #Hashtag Be Popular Tomorrow?" *Proceedings of the 35th International ACM SIGIR Conference on Research and Development in Information Retrieval* (August 12–16, 2012): 1173–4.

Lukács, Georg. *History and Class Consciousness: Studies in Marxist Dialectics*. Trans. Rodney Livingstone. Cambridge, MA: MIT Press, 1971.

Martin, Ernst. *Die Schreibmaschine und ihre Entwicklungsgeschichte*. Aachen: Basten, 1949; repr. 2003.

Merz, Sebastian. *#Hashtag-Marketing: How You Can Find Readers and Customers with Hashtag Marketing*. Berlin: Sebastian Merz, 2015.

Messina, Chris. "Groups for Twitter; or A Proposal for Twitter Tag Channels." *Factory Joe* (August 25, 2007): https://factoryjoe.com/2007/08/25/groups-for-twitter-or-a-proposal-for-twitter-tag-channels.

Mottahedeh, Negar. *#Iranelection: Hashtag Solidarity*

and the Transformation of Online Life. Stanford University Press, 2015.

Nichols, Pamela. "Hashtag Marketing: How to Use Hashtags that Fit Your Brand." *Blue Fountain Media* (October 1, 2017): www.bluefountainmedia.com/blog/hashtag-marketing-for-your-brand.

Orchard, Leslie Michael. "Sticky Tags for Twitter?" *oxDECAFBAD* (August 22, 2007): https://decafbad.com/blog/2007/08/22/sticky-tags-for-twitter.

Pandell, Lexi. "An Oral History of the #Hashtag." *Wired* (May 19, 2017): www.wired.com/2017/05/oral-history-hashtag.

Penny, Joel. *The Citizen Marketer: Promoting Political Opinion in the Social Media Age*. New York: Oxford University Press, 2017.

Peters, Isabella. *Folksonomies: Indexing and Retrieval in Web 2.0*. Berlin: De Gruyter, 2009.

Posch, L., C. Wagner, P. Singer, and M. Strohmaier. "Meaning as Collective Use: Predicting Semantic Hashtag Categories on Twitter." *Proceedings of the 22nd International Conference on World Wide Web Companion* (May 13–17, 2013): http://markusstrohmaier.info/documents/2013_MSM2013_Hashtag_Pragmatics.pdf.

Rambukkana, Nathan. "From #RaceFail to #Ferguson: The Digital Intimacies of Race-Activist

Hashtag Publics." In *Hashtag Publics: The Power and Politics of Discursive Networks*. Ed. Nathan Rambukkana. New York: Peter Lang, 2015, 29–46.

Rambukkana, Nathan. "#Introduction: Hashtags as Technosocial Events." In *Hashtag Publics: The Power and Politics of Discursive Networks*. Ed. Nathan Rambukkana. New York: Peter Lang, 2015, 1–10.

Rankl, Josef. "Hashtag Marketing." *EMarCon* (September 16, 2013): https://emarcon.de/hashtag-marketing.

Roloff, Heinrich. *Lehrbuch der Sachkatalogisierung*. 3rd edn. Munich: Verlag Dokumentation, 1968.

Salter, Kendall. "The Trouble with Tags: Seeking Mark Protection for Corporate Branded Hashtags – More Trouble than It's Worth." *Journal of Corporation Law* 43 (2018): 699–713.

Scheible, Jeff. *Digital Shift: The Cultural Logic of Punctuation*. Minneapolis: University of Minnesota Press, 2015.

Singh, Sava Saheli. "Hashtagging #HigherEd." In *Hashtag Publics: The Power and Politics of Discursive Networks*. Ed. Nathan Rambukkana. New York: Peter Lang, 2015, 267–72.

Smith, Gene. *Tagging: People-Powered Metadata for the Social Web*. Berkeley: New Riders, 2008.

Sohn-Rethel, Alfred. *Warenform und Denkform.* Frankfurt am Main: Suhrkamp, 1978.

Solon, Olivia. "US Olympic Committee Bullying Unofficial Sponsors Who Use Hashtags." *The Guardian* (July 22, 2016): www.theguardian.com/ sport/2016/jul/22/us-olympic-committee-bullying- unofficial-sponsors-hashtags.

Spieler, Karl-Heinz. *Zur Theorie des Schlagwortkatalogs.* Berlin: Deutscher Bibliotheksverband, 1975.

Stählin, Agnes. "Kleine Sprachlehre des Schlagwort- katalogs." In *Festschrift Eugen Stollreither zum 75. Geburtstage gewidmet von Fachgenossen, Schülern, Freunden.* Ed. Fritz Redenbacher. Erlangen: Universitätsbibliothek, 1950, 333–44.

Stählin, Agnes, and Roswitha Poll. *Regeln für den Schlagwortkatalog "Erlanger Regelwerk".* Munich: Verlag Dokumentation, 1977.

Turner, Julia. "#InPraiseOfTheHashtag." *New York Times Magazine* (November 2, 2012): www. nytimes.com/2012/11/04/magazine/in-praise-of- the-hashtag.html.

Tsur, O., and A. Rappoport. "What's in a Hashtag? Content Based Prediction of the Spread of Ideas in Microblogging Communities." *Proceedings of the Fifth ACM International Conference on Web Search and Data Mining* (February 8–12, 2012):

http://citeseerx.ist.psu.edu/viewdoc/download?doi
=10.1.1.221.5033&rep=rep1&type=pdf.

Von Wyss, Wilhelm. *Über den Schlagwortkatalog: Mit Regeln für die Stadtbibliothek Zürich*. Zurich: Stadtbibliothek, 1909.

Wasserman, Todd. "Six Successful Twitter Hashtag Campaigns." *Mashable* (March 23, 2012): https://mashable.com/2012/03/23/twitter-hashtag-campaigns/?europe=true#R7C3l.0EJSqE.

Wolter, Beatrice. *Deutsche Schlagwörter zur Zeit des Dreßigjährigen Krieges*. Frankfurt am Main: Peter Lang, 2000.

Wülfing, Wulf. *Schlagworte des Jungen Deutschland: Mit einer Einführung in die Schlagwortforschung*. Berlin: Erich Schmidt, 1982.

Yang, Guobin. "Narrative Agency in Hashtag Activism: The Case of #BlackLivesMatter." *Media and Communication* 4 (2016): 13–17.

Zappavigna, Michele. *Discourse of Twitter and Social Media: How We Use Language to Create Affiliation on the Web*. London: Sydney Bloomsbury, 2015.

Zappavigna, Michele. "Searchable Talk: The Linguistic Functions of Hashtags." *Social Semiotics* 25 (2015): 274–91.